Harry Taylor

What is Literature?

Focusing on the nature of literature, and primarily its relationship with human identity and contemporary society

GRIN Verlag

Bibliografische Information der Deutschen Nationalbibliothek:

Die Deutsche Bibliothek verzeichnet diese Publikation in der Deutschen National-
bibliografie; detaillierte bibliografische Daten sind im Internet über http://dnb.d-
nb.de/ abrufbar.

Dieses Werk sowie alle darin enthaltenen einzelnen Beiträge und Abbildungen
sind urheberrechtlich geschützt. Jede Verwertung, die nicht ausdrücklich vom
Urheberrechtsschutz zugelassen ist, bedarf der vorherigen Zustimmung des Verla-
ges. Das gilt insbesondere für Vervielfältigungen, Bearbeitungen, Übersetzungen,
Mikroverfilmungen, Auswertungen durch Datenbanken und für die Einspeicherung
und Verarbeitung in elektronische Systeme. Alle Rechte, auch die des auszugsweisen
Nachdrucks, der fotomechanischen Wiedergabe (einschließlich Mikrokopie) sowie
der Auswertung durch Datenbanken oder ähnliche Einrichtungen, vorbehalten.

Imprint:

Copyright © 2010 GRIN Verlag GmbH
Druck und Bindung: Books on Demand GmbH, Norderstedt Germany
ISBN: 978-3-656-35273-0

GRIN - Your knowledge has value

Der GRIN Verlag publiziert seit 1998 wissenschaftliche Arbeiten von Studenten, Hochschullehrern und anderen Akademikern als eBook und gedrucktes Buch. Die Verlagswebsite www.grin.com ist die ideale Plattform zur Veröffentlichung von Hausarbeiten, Abschlussarbeiten, wissenschaftlichen Aufsätzen, Dissertationen und Fachbüchern.

Visit us on the internet:

http://www.grin.com/

http://www.facebook.com/grincom

http://www.twitter.com/grin_com

Harry Taylor

What is Literature?

This essay focuses on the nature of literature, and primarily its relationship with
human identity and contemporary society. The focal element of the inquiry will be the
consideration of literature functioning as a cynosural social conscience, and the extent
to which it defines, affects and reflects collaborative social identity whilst remaining a
non-cognisant 'entity' in its own right. For the purposes of this investigation, the
multi-faceted term 'literature' will be comprised of three main aspects – the author,
the reader and society. In order to conduct said inquiry, several key elements of
literature will be considered, primarily: the role of contemporary society as the
material which provides the author with his muse, the author as a channel for the
societal zeitgeist, and the role of the reader as an interpreter of the medium. In
addition, the pertinence of literature with regard to the human search for a unique
identity will also be examined.

Camilo Jose Cela, the Spanish Nobel Laureate, said that "literature is the
denunciation of the times in which one lives" (Cela; 1942). In this respect, Cela is
perhaps stressing the role of literature as an entity with a defined agenda, and as such
is implying a purpose to works of literature. If an essential role of literature can
indeed be considered a criticism of the society within which it was created, then the
influence of an author is not only inevitable, but essential. It would imply an ulterior
agenda on behalf of the author to move distinctly away from the morally didactic 'art
for arts sake' principles of Aestheticism – instead directing criticism at the society in
which the author is resident. This objective view of literature was soon to become
somewhat outdated with the development of twentieth-century New Criticism (as will
later be examined). The question is then raised as to whether literature is indeed an
expression of the author or an outpouring of social, political and cultural revelation –
an unconscious attempt by the author to recruit the reader into the societal zeitgeist. In
this light, literature would perhaps be considered not so much a direct denunciation of
society, but an addition to it: "Literature adds to reality, it does not simply describe it.
It enriches the necessary competencies that daily life requires and provides; and in
this respect, it irrigates the deserts that our lives have already become" (C.S. Lewis;).
This suggests an alternative to the persuasive agenda of certain pieces of literature

that could perhaps be seen as an attempt to recruit the reader to an opinion held by the author. Is society itself therefore capable of informing the reader? Alexander Solzhenitsyn wrote that "literature that is not the breath of contemporary society, that dares not warn in time against threatening moral and social dangers... does not deserve the name of literature... it is only a façade" (Solzhenitsyn; 1969). This statement vigorously depicts what Solzhenitsyn considers to be the primary role of literature; to be the "breath of contemporary society" is evidently the demand being made of literature in this instance. Although Solzhenitsyn was writing in reference to the Soviet state, the application of his comment in wider context is undeniable. The notion that literature should be a reflection of contemporary society is an obvious and ever-present one. If it fails to fulfil this requirement expected of it, then it is merely (according to Solzhenitsyn) a 'façade' of deception which serves only to conceal the nature of the society which it purports to unmask. If this is indeed the intention of literature, then the role of the author also becomes clear. If literature is a mirror being held up to society, then the author – the 'creator' of said literature - is surely the person holding the mirror. This metaphor is, however, forcibly rejected by many, who describe it as "ancient... shattered and discarded [by] postmodern literature and critical theory" (Graff; 1979). If this is indeed the case, then what *is* the role of the author in the function and creation of literature? Is it to act as a channel – translating and packaging the very identity of contemporary society into verbiage capable of reaching out and speaking to the reader? From this perspective, the content and purpose of a piece of literature becomes something proposed not necessarily by the creator of the work, but by the society presented within it. When Ginsberg wrote *Howl*, he was encouraged to write with no restrictions and to do so with spontaneity and without consideration (Ginsberg; *Journals Mid-Fifties: 1954-1958*. Ed. Gordon Ball. HarperCollins, 1995). The poem that subsequently emerged was a savage and uninhibited protest against contemporary America, Ginsberg's own animalistic 'howl' of raw emotion. Following the first public reading of the poem, Michael McClure wrote: "Ginsberg read on to the end of the poem, which left us standing in wonder, or cheering and wondering, but knowing at the deepest level that a barrier had been broken, that a human voice and body had been hurled against the harsh wall of America..." (www.poets.org; From the Academy of American Poets: *Allen Ginsberg*). The freedom with which Ginsberg created *Howl* is particularly evident in the metre of the poem – each line is measured by a single breath. In doing so, Ginsberg seems to weakening the boundary between that which is deliberately delivered by the author in accordance with the accepted medium and that which is a direct and pure outpouring of the social conscience delivered by the uninhibited author of literature. The famous opening lines aptly demonstrate Ginsberg's ability to convey desperation and the primal outpourings of emotion the poem is renowned for: "I saw the best minds of my generation destroyed by madness, starving hysterical naked, / dragging themselves through the negro streets at dawn looking for an angry fix, / angelheaded hipsters burning for the ancient heavenly connection to the starry dynamo in the machinery of night" (Ginsberg; Howl). *Howl* was a brutal and unrepentant declaration of a generation unsatisfied by the society it found itself existing in. The frequent unashamed references to sex and drugs resulted in the much-publicised obscenity charges brought against the poem's publisher, perhaps confirming the very nature of the society howled at by Ginsberg – that which attempts to repress a conventionally immoral and obscene publication. Oscar Wilde wrote that "the books that the world calls immoral are the books that show the world its own shame" (Wilde; *The Picture of Dorian Gray*), and in this respect the statement is most certainly pertinent. However, despite the unwaveringly constant tirade of profanity, the publisher of *Howl* won the case brought against them in the obscenity trial of 1957 due to the judge deeming the poem to be of "redeeming social importance". *Howl* is being presented to a society that is forced to recognise itself in Ginsberg's poetry, the subsequent introspection of the reader resulting in the birth of the beat generation and recognition of the force of such unbridled creative spontaneity. In this respect, *Howl* as a literary exploit is expressive of the identity of contemporary society, and as such affirms the role of society as the primary element behind the creation and perseverance of literature. It is also only through literature that society is given a coherent identity, as in no other way is the reader presented with an assessment of such clarity and startling insight. In order for this critical reception to take place, however, an author is required to bridge the gap between society and reader.

It therefore seems undeniable that society influences the author in a highly significant way. The author cannot fail but be inspired by what they observe in the chaotic miasma formed by the political, cultural and social movements of their contemporary world. The means by which an author is capable of processing the input of society for digestion by the reader, however, are somewhat ambivalent. The role of the author is also cast into question, and even the very definition of an author is questionable. The issue of the author's identity is subsequently raised – is the author a valid interpretive entity, or merely a mouthpiece utilised by contemporary society to proclaim its own identity? The basic definition of an author is initially a straightforward one: an individual who creates a work of literature for a reader. In light of the assessment of society's role, the author's role seems similarly simple: to observe the varied nuances and activities of society – indeed, its nature – and to portray the identity of society in such a way that the reader can comprehend it. However, these seemingly self-evident definitions are rendered wholly unsuitable once alternative perspectives are taken into consideration. Roland Barthes neatly summarises the fundamental grounding of New Criticism by removing the consideration of any biographical or historical information whatsoever: "there is no time other than that of the enunciation, and every text is eternally written *here and now*" (Barthes; *The Death of the Author*; 315). If this is the case, then any role previously held by the author is now redundant. The sole purpose of the author is now only to provide himself as a palette with which society can create the literary work that is an intimate reflection of itself. This was put rather succinctly by Umberto Eco when he wrote "the author should die once he has finished writing so as not to trouble the path of the text" (Eco; from Postscript to *The Name of the Rose*; 1984). The death of the author is the chief concern of Barthes' essay, with the nullification of the creative force permitting the literary work to exist independently of the author's own interpretation of society. Eco also writes "a narrator should not supply interpretations of his work; otherwise he would not have written a novel, which is a machine for generating interpretations" (Eco; from Postscript to *The Name of the Rose*; 1984). This notion of literature as "a machine for generating interpretations" is a fascinating one, as it simultaneously permits the unique perspectives of each individual reader whilst acknowledging the role of the author as someone who must not colour their work with any hint of persuasive coherency. This raises pertinent questions regarding the nature of the author: does 'death' imply lack of identity, or merely an irrelevant one? The practise of an author to include some aspect of their identity (however minute) within a work of literature that they have produced in one that is perhaps inextricably rooted in the creation of a text. Woolf is perhaps acknowledging the

4

impossibility of complete distinction between the author and their work when she wrote that "somewhere, everywhere, now hidden, now apparent in whatever is written down, is the form of a human being. If we seek to know him, are we idly occupied?" (Woolf; *A Room of One's Own*; 143-144). This suggests a somewhat inevitable element of the authorial identity within any work, and therefore clarifies the role of the author in the definition and nature of literature. In the creation of such a work, the author unavoidably deposits a fraction of their own being within it, immortalising a fragment of their identity as an element inseparable from the piece of literature. In the novel *Absolute Beginners*, MacInnes' narrator asserts the significance of literature as something more than "just a thing… just *books*" (MacInnes; *Absolute Beginners*; 59) when he informs the reader that he was taught what he considers the nature of books as "somebody else's mind opened up for me to look into" (MacInnes; 59). This somewhat reductive approach to literature is nevertheless a partially accurate one when considered in accordance with the notion that the author is the very vessel which contains the elements of society concerned in a specific work. This strengthens the unavoidable indication that not only is the author (in a sense) inseparable from literature, but that society is dependent on the author as a means to interpret the contemporary zeitgeist for the reader. The identity of the author is therefore defined in terms of his 'death' – only through the reader's deliberate emancipation of the author from the work can the society being portrayed by the author be examined as an independent entity. The author then gains identity as the means of presenting literature to the reader free from biographical discolouration: "it is language which speaks, not the author" (Barthes, (1968), "The Death of the Author", *Image, Music, Text*). It is, however, the reader that interprets this language – an indisputably essential element of the literary process.

The nature of the reader is somewhat easier to define than that of the author, as it is undeniably an essential and ever-required facet of literature. If it is assumed that the role of the reader is to recognise and appreciate literature, it can also be surmised that the internalisation of said literature is a vital aspect of literary comprehension and appreciation. This does, however, present several problems – most notably with the issue of identity. The comprehension of literature with regard to the identity of the reader is an element of two parts. The first of these is literature as a means of establishing ones own unique identity separate from that being presented in the literary work. Thomas Carlyle once stated that "the best effect of any book is that it excites the reader to self-activity" – a claim with specific pertinence to the purpose of literature as a creator of identity. In MacInnes' novel *Absolute Beginners*, the narrator claims a fascination with books that sets him apart from his peers. He realises that the most important moments in his literary education and experience were that the topics he was learning about "had some actual value to you personally" and that in order to internalise knowledge gleaned from external sources, one must "[make] it part of your own experience" (MacInnes; 59). Despite failing to elaborate any further with regard to this matter, the anonymous narrator proceeds to adopt a somewhat supercilious attitude towards his less well-read peers: "kids… those days… thought a book's an SF or a Western, if they thought it's anything". We see here an aspect of the narrator's persona that pursues education purely for the sake of appearing more intelligent. The narrator is clearly doing this in an attempt to construct his own unique identity and distinguish himself from society, pointedly trying to mark himself out as an autodidact whose comprehension of literary matters is far superior to that possessed by the contemporary demographic he is trying to escape. This emergence of the reader into a new identity populated by an enhanced relationship between society and himself is one that cannot be achieved in the presence of the author. Although the author's presentation of society is that which enables a degree of heightened comprehension in the reader, it is impossible for a new and unique identity to be constructed on the back of what may remain of the author's. As Barthes wrote, "the birth of the reader must be at the cost of the death of the author" (Barthes). The relationship between the reader and the author is therefore a careful one. The reader must ensure that he does not so readily adopt aspects of the literary work into his identity, as this could potentially threaten the individuality nurtured by the unguided perusal of literature. If the author was to construct his work in a more overt manner, such as the clear and distinct views voiced with comparatively scant coherency (in the traditional sense) in Ginsberg's *Howl*, then the reader would be responsible for subjecting each strata of opinion to consideration, lest he adopt the principles of the author. In this way, it would be easy for the reader to have one's perceptions and opinions altered by either the currents of society within the literary work, or the voice of the author himself: "reading is equivalent to thinking with someone else's head instead of with one's own" (Schopenhauer).

The relationship between the reader and society is also an interesting one. It could be argued that potentially the whole population of a society are the 'readers' of works which (intentionally or otherwise) reflect the reality of their own lives. If the reader is influenced by the identity of society through literature and applies it to their own personal 'unique' identity, then each 'reader' is simply adopting the same fragments of identity as one another. If society is comprised of 'readers' all striving for individuality, all from the same source, then a subtle irony is revealed: striving for 'uniqueness' serves only to make such individuals more similar. This is demonstrated to some degree in *Absolute Beginners*, where the conviction of the anonymous narrator that casual reading of a few books is a suitable substitute for formal education is synonymous with the widespread teenage belief that this is sufficient to propel oneself over the ramparts of Philistinism and into a new identity considered far more sophisticated and mature. Similarly, the number of people in *Absolute Beginners* adopting the bohemian lifestyle seems ironically widespread, considering that it is presented by the narrator as a means of distinguishing oneself from established social expectations. In this respect, the unique identity being pursued by the teenagers in *Absolute Beginners* is foiled by the significantly substantial swathe of society that attempts to emulate the same practise.

Literature has created a loop of dependency, with the reader, the author, and society influencing each other and preventing the formation of a truly unique social identity in either individual respect. It could therefore be surmised that the connectivity and interdependency of each of these key elements (society, the author, and the reader) could potentially appear to result in something of a circular cause and consequence fallacy (a chicken-or-the-egg 'fallacy dilemma'). None can have purpose without the other elements of literature being simultaneously present. The only aspect of these facets with any true identity is perhaps 'society', as works of literature suffice as indicators of the zeitgeist, as memes of the nature of contemporary society. The death of the author and the subsequent fulfilment of the outstanding role by language has the dangerous potential for over-mystification of literature, and ensuing loss of authorial identity. While the usefulness of a critical approach encompassing historical, biographical and cultural elements of literary composition is often overstated, it can still be useful. For example, a reader attempting to digest a work with origins in Ancient Greece would be hindered by the lack of explanatory footnotes on contemporary customs and culture – rendering it a poorer literary experience on the whole. The work must surely be considered with clarity by the reader in order to ensure preservation of the intent in its creation. Rushdie writes: "the liveliness of literature lies in its exceptionality, in being the individual, idiosyncratic vision of one human being, in which, to our delight and great surprise, we may find our own vision reflected" (Rushdie, 2001). Literature, then, is the process of linguistic representation and progression as the author transcribes a perception of contemporary society and passes the pieces of language on to the reader. It is an unceasingly regenerative accumulation and expression of social identity that requires each of the three key elements of literature to appropriately represent a reflection of humanity.

Bibliography

- MacInnes, C; 1959; *Absolute Beginners*; London; Allison and Busby
- Lewis, C.S; http://www.tc.umn.edu/~burc0050/quotes_lewis.html (accessed 29/03/2010)
- Cela, C.J; http://www.eclectica.org/v12n4/umez.html (accessed 12/04/2010)
- Solzhenitsyn, A; 1969; http://www.jstor.org/pss/40126747 (accessed 12/04/2010)
- Graff, G; 1979; *Literature Against Itself: Literary Ideas in Modern Society*; http://www.fglaysher.com/literature_against_itself.html (accessed on 01/05/2010)
- Ginsberg, A; 1995; *Journals Mid-Fifties: 1954-1958*. Ed. Gordon Ball; HarperCollins
- McClure, M; www.poets.org; From the Academy of American Poets: *Allen Ginsberg*; accessed on 02/05/2010
- Ginsberg, A; 2009; *Howl, Caddish and Other Poems*; London; Penguin
- Wilde, O; 2004; *The Picture of Dorian Gray*; London; Longman; Rev Ed edition
- Eco, U; 1984; from Postscript to *The Name of the Rose*; http://www.guardian.co.uk/books/booksblog/2010/jan/13/death-of-the-author (accessed 28/04/2010)
- Woolf, V; 2002, *A Room of One's Own*; London; Penguin Classics; New Ed edition
- *Modern Criticism and Theory – A Reader*; 2008; Roland Barthes: "The Death of the Author"; Pearson Education Limited
- Schopenhauer, A; http://linguaspectrum.com/quotations/by_author_english.php?quoteoftheday_author=Arthur%20Schopenhauer (accessed on 28/04/2010)
- Rushdie, S; 1998; *The Satanic Verses*; Consortium Inc; New edition